My First Advent Calendar

High Contrast Baby for Newborns

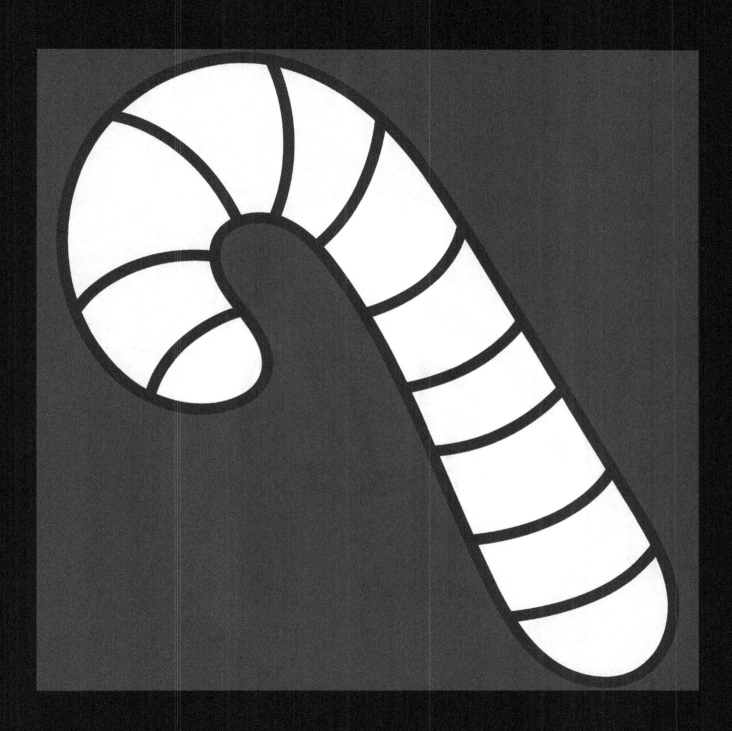

Enjoyed this book?
Please consider leaving a review

Would you like to receive 24 free flashcards? Scan the QR code below!

www.talentedtreasurespublishing.com

Made in the USA
Middletown, DE
27 November 2022

16135760R00031